THIS THING CALLED

TREATMENT

THE ORIGIN OF SPIRITUAL MIND TREATMENT

BY REV. RITA ANDRIELLO-FEREN

First published in 2011 as *Trained Thought is More Powerful Than Untrained Thought: The Origin of Spiritual Mind Treatment*.

Submitted to Reverend James J. Mellon, Founding Spiritual Director of the NoHo Arts Center for New Thought, North Hollywood, CA in partial fulfillment of the requirements for the License of MINISTER OF SCIENCE MIND: April 4, 2011.

Cover and Interior Design by Jonathan Zenz

Second Printing 2017

10 9 8 7 6 5 4 3 2

Author's Note: With regard to quotes and other instances where the masculine pronoun or noun is used, it is understood that the meaning encompasses all of humankind, both male and female.

TABLE OF CONTENTS

FOREWORD

The New Thought Movement brought to the world a holistic approach to the oneness with Universal Power, self-healing and the creation of our best life. Rev. Rita has brought history, heart and the practicality of this movement, and specifically the work of Dr. Ernest Holmes, to you dear reader in a clear, heart-filled, and concise manner. It is my great pleasure to introduce Rev. Rita's treatise on the origins of Holmes' philosophy and the practical affirmative prayer he called Spiritual Mind Treatment. It is as much a powerful enlightening story as treatment is a Divinely Powered method of healing and connecting to our best Self.

Rev. Jay Willick
The New Thought Guy
Los Angeles, August 2012

CHAPTER 1:
INTRODUCTION

"Through reading, discussion, experimentation, Ernest Holmes developed a mental healing technique similar in some aspects to the healing practices of Christian Science.

He called his technique 'Spiritual Mind Treatment.'"[1]

Originally published as a thesis paper, this book poses the question: how did Ernest Holmes develop the mental healing technique that Religious Scientists know today as the five steps of Spiritual Mind Treatment? The writer of this paper suggests that there is no direct route written that answers this question, so the writer will attempt to give a conclusion. In order to arrive at this conclusion, this paper will explore how healers and philosophers including, but not limited to, Jesus, Anton Mesmer, Ralph Waldo Emerson, Thomas Troward, Mary Baker Eddy, and Emma Curtis Hopkins influenced Ernest Holmes.

In turn, by researching what Ernest Holmes gleaned from these spiritual geniuses throughout time, the writer will attempt to create a roadmap from the theoretical to the practical technique known as the Five Steps of Spiritual Mind Treatment, or as Ernest Holmes defines it: "...the time, process and method necessary to the changing of our thought. Treatment is clearing the thought of negation, of doubt and fear,

and causing it to perceive the ever-presence of God."[2]

CHAPTER 2:
WHO WAS ERNEST SHURTLEFF HOLMES?

It would not be possible to discuss Ernest Holmes' technique for healing known as Spiritual Mind Treatment, without an overview of his life. His thirst for knowledge and his ever-questioning mind brought him to a place of faith in, and understanding of, the Power of the Universe and how to use it. His whole ministry was based on one statement that he spoke and wrote over and over: "There is a Power for Good in the Universe and you can use it." Anyone who sets out to read about this great, yet humble man can see he most definitely used this Power throughout his life.

Ernest Shurtleff Holmes was born in Lincoln, Maine on January 21, 1887. His parents were William Nelson Holmes, a farmer, and Anna Heath. His family was poor and moved many times throughout his childhood. Ernest Holmes and his family were avid readers and studiers of the Bible. Although Ernest was brought up in a conservative and harsh Christian religion of his time, from a very early age, his parents taught him that God was not cruel and judgmental, but loving and kind. He was taught that he was not a "worm of the dust," but a son of God. Later, these two tenets would become part of the philosophy he would develop called the Science of Mind; and he would impart this wisdom to the world.

Ernest received very little formal education. He felt the need to be free of school, so he left school in his late teens, and instead became a student of life itself. He was an avid reader of the greatest authors of all time. He had a passion for nature and spent much of his time communing with it. He questioned everything. In fact, as a child he became known as the "eternal question mark."[3]

As his mind was expanding, so did his geographical exploration. He took his destiny into his own hands and moved from Maine to the city of Boston, Massachusetts in 1905 at the age of 18. There he lived and worked with his relatives and spent all his free time studying the great philosophers, poets and writers. His thirst for knowledge was unquenchable. He attended church with his aunt, but he did not believe in its dualistic teachings. He could not understand a God who had a dualistic nature. Thus, he didn't believe in Heaven and Hell. He continued to question everything and to find his answers in nature, books and in the solace of his own soul.

He was searching for something he had not quite found until 1907, when he was visiting his brother,

William, and picked up a copy of Ralph Waldo Emerson's Essays. "Reading Emerson is like drinking water to me,"[4] he wrote. The philosophy written in Emerson's *Self-Reliance* resonated to Ernest Holmes' intuitive knowledge that he was his own spiritual authority.

In 1914, at the age of 25, Ernest Holmes moved again to join his mother and brother, Fenwicke, in Venice, California. He assisted Fenwicke, who was a minister at his own Congregationalist church. At the same time, Ernest was working for the city of Venice as a playground director and a purchasing manager. It was at this time Ernest Holmes discovered the writings of Thomas Troward. Troward was the second pillar in Ernest's quest for truth. Ernest Holmes found Troward's writing to be captivating for both the heart and the mind. He was so excited about Troward and felt so akin to his philosophy that he began speaking to small groups on Troward's book *The Edinburgh Lectures on Mental Science*.

Near the same time, Ernest Holmes attended a public speaking class, where he became interested in the works of Mary Baker Eddy and Christian Science. He resonated to the Christian Science method of prayer. However, he soon left Mary Baker Eddy behind for Christian D. Larson and Ralph Waldo Trine, two New Thought writers. Fenwicke and Ernest started taking a correspondence course offered by Christian D. Larson.

It was at this time that Ernest and his brother

Fenwicke actively began a mental healing ministry. The brothers opened a mental healing sanitarium in Long Beach and the Southern California Metaphysical Institute in Los Angeles. In 1915 Ernest Holmes gave his first mental healing lecture and the brothers began writing their periodical Uplift.

In 1917, Ernest Holmes' Sunday lectures began at the Strand Theater in LA. He attracted large crowds for the lectures, healing sessions and classes. Ernest Holmes was soon ordained as a minister of Divine Science in Seattle. No matter where he spoke, he filled the house to capacity. And so, he moved to a larger and larger space, until he was speaking to well over two thousand people at a time on Sundays.

In 1919, Ernest Holmes published his very first book, Creative Mind. Almost immediately following this publication he wrote and published Creative Mind and Success.

In 1924, Ernest Holmes studied with Emma Curtis Hopkins, the mystic and teacher of teachers. Ernest Holmes said she was the greatest mystic he had ever met. It is said that Hopkins more than likely inspired him to establish his own institute.

In between lecturing to larger and larger audiences and all his studying, Ernest Holmes was formally developing the Science of Mind philosophy. He wrote the book The Science of Mind. This book became the textbook of Religious Science. First published in 1926, it was revised in 1938.

Soon after, those closest to Ernest asked him to set up a formal organization/church. At first he refused. He thought men should think for themselves and did not want to tell people what to do. In *That Was Ernest*, Reginald Armor wrote, "Ernest was thinking bigger than a church or denomination or a religion...Very early there existed in Ernest's thought a world training center for the universal Sonship of man, under the universal parentage of the One, no matter by what name this One was called, where people of all faiths, all creeds, all colors, all kinds of speech, all areas of learning could be one in the feeling of oneness that they had with the Infinite."[5]

So, eventually Ernest Holmes agreed to set up an organization and the Institute of Religious Science and the School of Philosophy was born in 1927. However, it wasn't until 1953 that the Institute became the Church of Religious Science.

On October 23, 1927 Ernest Holmes married Hazel Durkee Foster. She was very influential with the Los Angeles elite and Hollywood scene and she attracted many of these influential people to her husband and his teachings. His speaking, teaching and healing ministry continued to grow.

In 1954 due to conflicts in the hierarchy of his organization and its distribution of power and responsibilities, the teaching institute split from the church organization and became two separate entities. It was said by those closest to Ernest Holmes that there was a big difference in him after 'The Split.' Fletcher

Harding noted that "Ernest was never the same after the fighting, quarreling and dissension that led to the split."[6]

Compounding this disappointment, his beloved wife Hazel made her transition on May 21, 1957. After Hazel's death, Ernest began to lose his zest for life.

"Her death in 1957 had a major impact on him. 'It was very hard on Ernest,' recalls Frieda Grinton. 'It was the first time I saw Ernest almost fall apart... When she left, it was a tremendous shock to his whole thinking process. After she was gone,' Elaine St. Johns recalls, 'Ernest just wanted to go. He wanted to join her'"[7]

And, so he did. A man whom doctors found healthy all his life began to deteriorate quickly. Ernest Holmes made his transition on April 7, 1960.

On February 12, 1959, in one of his last speeches, he said:

"There are many wonderful religions in the world. We are not better than the others. We are not more spiritual. We are not more evolved. We are not more anything, other than this one thing: we have co-joined our consciousness with the eternal verity of the Universe, that everlasting and eternal Father of life, and the Mother of all creation forever begetting the Only-Begotten, is begetting Him in us, right now. And that the word of our mouth is a word of Truth in such degree as it emulates and embodies the Truth

which sanctifies the word to its unique service
of healing not only of the sick, but the poor in
heart."[8]

The great mystic Ernest Holmes passed from the earthly plane, but not without leaving man with a practical tool that could be used to heal one's life. Through a lifetime of reading and synthesizing everything he read, Ernest Holmes came to the conclusion that man was one with the Divine and that he was governed by his use of the Law of Cause and Effect.

Ernest Holmes knew that the power of man's thoughts is what moves the great Law of Life to his detriment or betterment. He knew the Law was always working through man's conscious or subconscious direction. Therefore, if man was to use this Power, he'd better learn to use his mind constructively, to control the power of his subconscious. "Trained thought is more powerful than untrained thought," he wrote.[9]

Ernest Holmes left the world with a way for man to train his thought: Spiritual Mind Treatment. The next part of this book will piece together the many influential voices in Ernest Holmes' life and attempt to show the unique contribution each had upon the art and science of Spiritual Mind Treatment.

CHAPTER 3:
JESUS, THE GREAT EXAMPLE

"Let this mind be in you, which was also in
Christ Jesus." —*Philippians 2:5*

Although Religious Science does not embrace Jesus as a personal savior, the major goal of Religious Scientists is to live as the Christ Consciousness or at one with the Divine. Jesus the man is called 'Jesus the Christ' because he totally embodied Christ Consciousness.

Religious Science, if truly lived, embraces the truths that Jesus taught during his ministry as they are recorded in the Christian Bible. However, Ernest Holmes writes,

"The Bible does not tell us how to give a treatment. It is only within the last hundred years that the science which we are studying has been given to the world. It is not an old system of thought. The old systems of thought did contain the Truth, but one would never learn how to give

an effective mental treatment by studying them.
We would no more learn how to give a treatment
by studying the Bible, than we would learn how
to psycho-analyze a person."[10]

It would seem that Ernest Holmes was continually seeking throughout his study of all philosophies and teachers for a practical way to help man control his destiny. He knew there was a Power for Good in the Universe and man could use it! Would he find how to use it in the Bible? Reading the above quote, one might conclude that he at least was looking there. Although he did not find the practical method of treatment in the Bible, *The Science of Mind* text is filled with hundreds of references to Jesus and his curative powers. One might not be able to turn to Jesus and the Bible for the five step method of treatment, but Ernest Holmes received much from the teachings of Jesus that are cornerstones to the steps of Spiritual Mind treatment.

First is the Unity of God and man. Just as Jesus professed, "I and the Father are One"[11], the power of God as man is what makes Spiritual Mind Treatment effective. It is from this place that the practitioner is able to speak his word with authority. The practitioner must have the faith of God just as Jesus did.

Ernest Holmes writes, "The faith of God is very different from a faith in God. The faith of God IS God... Always in such a degree as this happens, a demonstration takes place."[12]

The basic tenet of Religious Science that is

reiterated over and over in The Science of Mind is, "It is done unto you as you believe." This most certainly is found in the Bible as the cornerstone of Jesus's teachings.

> *"And Jesus said unto the centurion, 'Go thy way; as thou hast believed, so be it done unto thee... Let it be done for you as you have believed.'"[13]*

Ernest Holmes quotes Jesus in numerous ways in order to expound on the power of belief in treatment. For example, he writes on page 38 of The Science of Mind, "AS MUCH AS WE CAN BELIEVE, will be done unto us."

Yes, belief is the whole basis of Science of Mind teaching and most certainly another cornerstone of Spiritual Mind Treatment.

> *"We come to understand, then, that the answer to prayer is in the prayer when it is prayed—the belief of the one praying sets in motion the Law of Love, which is the fundamental Law of the Universe."[14]*

Holmes further states,

> *"The person who speaks his word, releases it, but is filled with doubt and misgiving, as to whether it will ever be fulfilled, has his answer right then. The prayer will be answered but in reverse...All prayers are answered. They are answered according to the pattern of the individual's thinking and conviction of the time."[15]*

Ernest Holmes makes it very clear that belief is the backbone of Spiritual Mind Treatment. He could have only received this knowledge from the great example, Jesus.

Another cornerstone of Spiritual Mind Treatment is the power of the practitioner's word. In both the teachings of Jesus and throughout the Old Testament, the power of the word as being the power of God is most evident. It states in John 1:1, "In the beginning was the Word, and the Word was with God, and the Word was God."

Jesus the Christ spoke his word and all were healed. "Jesus reached out his hand and touched the man... He said, "Be clean!" And immediately the leprosy left him."[16]

Yes, the practitioner's word, backed by his belief, sets the Law of Mind in motion. One of the places Ernest Holmes gathered knowledge about the power of the word and the Law of Cause and Effect was the Bible.

In The Science of Mind, Holmes writes,

"From the beginning to end, in one way or another, the Bible teaches the Law of Cause and Effect, based upon the premise that the Universe is a spiritual system, that man is included in this spiritual system, that the Infinite creates by the power of Its word or the contemplation of Its consciousness..."[17]

The fourth step of treatment is Gratitude. Again, one can turn to Jesus as the great example. There are numerous instances throughout his teachings and miracles where he gives thanks. In fact, Jesus never began anything without giving thanks. For example, in the miracle of the loaves and fishes it is written, "He told the crowd to sit down on the ground. When he had taken the seven loaves and given thanks, he broke them and gave them to his disciples to set before the people, and they did so."[18]

In summary, although there is not a definite formula in the Bible for Spiritual Mind Treatment, it cannot be denied that the Jesus was indeed the great way-shower of the power of spiritual healing. Ernest Holmes was a student of the Bible. He was a student of Jesus. Ernest Holmes makes hundreds of references to Jesus as the great example throughout all his writings.

It is concluded by the writer that Ernest Holmes was taking lots and lots of mental notes while he was reading the Bible. What made Jesus so powerful? And, why did he tell man he could do more? Ernest Holmes took what Jesus said very, very seriously. He was determined to do more and to make sure to pass it on in a way humanity could understand and use.

"Well did the Great Teacher say, *With what measure ye mete, it shall be measured to you again.* It is done unto us, but only as we believe."
Ernest Holmes
Living the Science of Mind

CHAPTER 4:
ANTON MESMER

A German physician with an interest in astronomy, Franz Anton Mesmer was born on May 23, 1734. His healing practice began based on the premise that "there was a natural energetic transference that occurred between all animated and inanimate objects that he called animal magnetism."[19]

Anton Mesmer claimed that the planets and solar system exuded rays that affected our bodies. His healing work included harnessing this power.

In the beginning of his practice, he harnessed this energy in magnetic tubes and placed it on the bodies of his patients. Eventually he did not need the magnetic tubes, affirming that he was a conduit for the energy. He healed through laying his hands on his patients. His treatment technique progressed further when he discovered he could affect the patient from another room. Thus, he began to speak with the patient to heal them and the concept of "mental suggestion" began.

The evolution of Mesmer's practices finally led the Scottish surgeon James Braid to develop what we now know as hypnosis. Braid himself did not associate himself with Mesmerism as he thought it was "preposterous."

Mesmer was an entertainer as well:

"Patients would sit in a circle in his salon holding hands, enveloped in the mystery, as the amazing healer would enter robed in some extravagant cape like a magical being of the highest order. As he let his will be known to his patients, the most amazing things would happen, such as cataleptic trances, hysterical laughter, and dervishlike dancing. At the end of these sessions the patients had hardly any recollection of what took place, and claimed to be healed." [20]

And thus our understanding of what it is to be "mesmerized." There was much controversy over Mesmer's work. He was accused of seducing patients and for the most part named a quack of sorts. The conclusion was that the magnetic fields did not exist, but that "any beneficial result from such a treatment was due to self-suggestion." [21]

In other words, as Charles Braden in his book Spirits in Rebellion wrote, "All that was necessary was to provoke a high state of expectancy in the patient." [22] And so, it was concluded that the cause of the trance lay not outside of but within the patient.

Animal Magnetism became Mesmerism, which led to the study of hypnosis. In turn, the study of hypnosis brought forth the study of the power of the subconscious mind, which most definitely acted below the conscious mind and could affect one's physical experience. It was determined that distressed mental states could affect the normal function of the body.

What can be gleaned from the work of Anton Mesmer as far as Ernest Holmes and Spiritual Mind Treatment is concerned? Ernest Holmes studied Mesmer. This writer concludes that more than likely his study of Mesmer gave Ernest Holmes more insight and momentum to continue to study the power of controlling the subconscious or subjective mind.

Although Ernest never advocated hypnosis, he understood the importance of controlling one's own subconscious through the use of the conscious mind. What he also might have gleaned from Mesmer was the openness of the subconscious mind to suggestion. This would have given Ernest Holmes more initiative to find a way for the individual to control his own subconscious or subjective mind, for, as he stated:

> *"The conscious mind is Spirit;*
>
> *the subjective mind is Law."*[23]

CHAPTER 5:
PHINEAS QUIMBY

In and around 1830, an inventor from Portland, Maine observed a Mesmerist performance. He decided there was something in this form of healing and began experimenting. This man eventually left Mesmerism and developed his own healing science. He became a well known mental healer throughout New England. His name was Phineas Parkhurst Quimby. He documented all his work in his manuscripts, which were later transcribed and edited by Horatio Dresser, who was healed by Quimby. The book is called The Quimby Manuscripts. His method of healing was called "The Science of Health."

From an early age, Quimby himself suffered from tuberculosis. Unhappy with many doctors' unsuccessful means of treatment and cure, he embarked on his own path of discovery. This led Quimby to realize the power of the mind over the effects of the body.

After studying and practicing Mesmerism, his

ideas were confirmed. The mind could influence the body. He began working with a clairvoyant, Lucius Burkmar. Lucius could fall into a trance and diagnose disease. He would prescribe medicines with no physical validity to the patient. The patient would take them, and the patient would be cured. Quimby and Lucius worked together healing those that came to them. Quimby eventually parted ways with Lucius, and developed and began practicing on his own healing technique. Quimby was said to have healed over 1,000 people a year for approximately 15 years.

Quimby believed that the two big enemies of Wisdom, or God, were priests and doctors. He believed priests and doctors were the main source of people's wrong beliefs, which in turn caused disease. Quimby knew if he could change a man's beliefs to Truth, he could cure him.

"He discovered that belief alone makes man sick and it is belief alone that heals. He spent the last years of his life in healing work through mental means alone and he became known as the 'Father of New Thought'"[24] in America.

Quimby wrote of his cure:

"A patient comes in to see Dr. Quimby. He (Dr. Quimby) renders himself absent to everything but the impression of the patient's feelings. These are quickly daguerreotyped on him. They contain no intelligence, but shadow forth a reflection of themselves which he looks at: this contains the disease as it appears to the patient.

Being confident that it is the shadow of a false idea, he is not afraid of it, but laughs at it. Then his feelings in regard to the disease, which are health and strength, are daguerreotyped on the receptive-plate of the patient, which also throws forth a shadow. The patient, seeing this shadow of the disease in a new light, gains confidence. This change of feeling is daguerreotyped on the doctor again, and this [new impression] also throws forth a shadow, and he sees the change and continues to treat it the same way. So the patient's feelings sympathize with his, the shadow grows dim, and finally light takes its place, and there is nothing left of the disease."[25]

Quimby believed that the healing technique he used was the same healing technique that Jesus used. He reiterated the teaching of Jesus in Matthew 8:13: "And Jesus said unto the centurion, 'Go thy way; and as thou hast believed so be it done unto thee.' And his servant was healed in the selfsame hour."

Ernest Holmes more than likely received much wisdom from studying Quimby's methods of assisting a patient in changing his beliefs. The whole Science of Mind philosophy is based on the premise that to change our life we must change our thinking or what we believe. This is the whole purpose of Spiritual Mind Treatment.

Ernest Holmes directs the practitioner:

"The Creative Medium is a medium only, never

a person. It is necessary that we understand this, because one of the first things a practitioner has to do is to separate the belief from the believer. From the standpoint of the spiritual man, disease, poverty, unhappiness, and misery, are neither person, place, nor thing."[26]

Ernest Holmes professed that the realization form of treatment was the ideal style of treatment. Realization means that the practitioner simply realizes the ever-presence of Perfect Spirit as the patient without an argument. However he also understood that sometimes more is needed to convince one's mind of the Truth. Therefore, he outlined the argumentative style or seven-step style of treatment, where the practitioner brings the condition into the treatment in order to neutralize it with the Truth.

There is a similarity between argumentative or seven step treatment and Quimby's technique. Quimby argued with the patient's erroneous thoughts of disease and convinced them of Truth or Wisdom.

Quimby wrote:

"...the trouble is in the mind, for the body is only the house for the mind to dwell in... If your mind has been deceived by some invisible enemy into a belief, you have put it into the form of a disease, with or without your knowledge. By my theory or truth I come in contact with your enemy and restore you to health and happiness."[27]

"The time will come when men and women shall heal all diseases with the words of their mouth."
Phineas Quimby

CHAPTER 6:
RALPH WALDO EMERSON

Ralph Waldo Emerson was a philosopher and essayist born and raised in New England. His father was Reverend William Emerson, a Unitarian minister. Emerson strayed from the religion of his father. He first expressed his own philosophy of "Transcendentalism" in his very first essay, "Nature," in 1836.

Transcendentalism was born from the works of German Philosopher Immanuel Kant. It brings in the Eastern belief system and teaches

"...that there is a higher reality and greater knowledge than that manifested in the human mind. It divides reality into a realm of spirit and a realm of matter, a basic premise of many of the great religions of the world."[28]

Ernest Holmes was visiting his brother William in 1907 when he found a copy of Emerson's essays. His brother Fenwicke said Ernest read the book in two days. Fenwicke wrote in Ernest's biography, "It was at that moment that life really began for Ernest Holmes. He had entered the foreground of the Idea."[29]

It was the idea of independence and nonconformity that Ernest really resonated to. No wonder! Ernest Holmes had been a nonconformist his whole life, questioning everyone and everything that came within his field of experience. "Be yourself," Emerson wrote,

"It is easy in the world to live after the world's opinion; it is easy in solitude to live after our own; but the great man is he who in the midst of the crowd keeps with perfect sweetness the independence of solitude."[30]

These words gave Ernest a spiritual freedom he'd never experienced before. He was dedicated to bring out the inner genius in all people. Ernest wrote,

"...reading Emerson for the first time, the first half-dozen lectures or essays, gave me a realization that in a certain sense every man has to interpret the universe in terms of his own thinking and personal relationships, and that in order to do it, he has to have faith and confidence in his own interpretation."[31]

Interestingly, at the time Ernest was studying Emerson, he was bothered by a throat irritation. Ernest came to understand that he was creating this physical ailment because of his concerns about other people's perceptions of the new thoughts he was imparting to the world through the use of his voice.

"Emerson taught me that I must have faith and confidence in my own interpretation of the universe and my relation to it."[32]

When Ernest embodied this concept, his throat irritations disappeared. In the essay the Over-Soul Emerson wrote,

"We live in succession, in division, in parts, in particles. Meantime within man is the soul of the whole; the wise silence; the universal beauty, to which every part and particle is equally related; the eternal ONE."

Ernest believed that all people shared a unity in the Divine Mind:

"There is but One Mind and One Law, which all people use, consciously or unconsciously, constructively or destructively: One Spirit, One Mind, One Law, One Substance…but many forms…"[33]

And so from Emerson, Holmes embodied these three ideas: We are our own Spiritual Authority, there is a Divine essence that expresses through everyone and unites everyone to each other, and also that there is a connection between our thoughts and what happens to us.

It is easy to translate these three things as more fuel for the development of Spiritual Mind Treatment. For example, the idea of the Divine Essence that expresses through all creation and unites all creation allows the practitioner to pray and affect the Universal Mind, which then affects the mind of his client if he is receptive. This is the core concept of absent treatment.

Being one's own Spiritual Authority reiterates man's oneness with God, the SELF, and gives each person the authority to control and be responsible for his own destiny.

The connection between man's thoughts and what happens to him gives way to the absolute Law of Cause and Effect and fuel for the importance of finding a way to control one's thoughts.

It can be concluded that Emerson's essays support the first two steps of Spiritual Mind Treatment: Recognition that God is all there is and our Unification or oneness with this Presence.

CHAPTER 7:
THOMAS TROWARD

Thomas Troward was born in 1847 in Punjab, India. His father was in the Indian Army; therefore he spent much of his early life in India. Troward was brought back to England at the age of 18 to attend school. He studied literature and received a degree in Law. It is said, even when he was practicing law, he always considered himself an artist and a painter.

In 1869, Troward went back to India and took the Civil Service Exam. He passed, and surprised everyone with the depth and originality of his answers on metaphysics. He eventually became a Divisional Judge in Punjab where he served for 25 years.

Troward was married twice and had six children. He loved to paint and to study the sacred books of all the Eastern religions. He studied all the Bibles including the Koran, Hindu scriptures and books of Raja Yoga. He even read the Jewish Bible in its original Hebrew.

Troward returned to England at the age of 55 and devoted himself to writing and painting. He wanted to develop a system of philosophy that gave peace of mind and the practical results of physical health and happiness to people. He began writing for the New Thought Expressions publication.

The Higher Thought Center of London immediately recognized him for his genius and ability to articulate that genius. He was invited to give a series of lectures at Queens Gate in Edinburgh, Scotland. Although he was considered a boring speaker, his profound wisdom did not go unnoticed.

Troward's books are filled with scientific jargon and a Christian bent from his upbringing in the Church of England. Sarah Ann, his second wife, helped publish his works after his death. She wrote in the forward of On the Psalms, "When he retired from the Bengal Civil Service in 1896, he decided to devote himself to three objects--the study of the Bible, writing his books, and painting pictures... He believed that the solution to all our problems was there (in the Bible) for those who read and meditated with minds at one with its Inspirer."

Thomas Troward made his transition in 1916. He is recognized as a contributing influence to Religious Science, the New Thought Movement in the U.S. and Great Britain, and also to the more liberal ideas of the Church of England.

Thomas Troward was more than a major influence

on the work of Ernest Holmes. When Ernest Holmes found the writings of Troward, he felt he had arrived home. He said,

> *"The thing I like about Troward is that he gives a scientific or logical explanation of whatever he claims. Take the idea of 'unity,' for example. He quotes from the ancient teachers of India, saying that it is impossible to have two infinities, for if there were two, neither of them could be infinite. Therefore, there is only one."* [34]

Ernest Holmes began his first public lectures in 1916 expounding on the Edinburgh Lectures. Ernest once said:

> *"Troward eclipsed anything I had ever read. In fact, I couldn't help saying to myself, 'This is exactly what I feel. This solves the problem of dualism. This is the Law.'"* [35]

Ernest Holmes liked the way Troward stated his case and then logically proved it. He liked the reasoning he brought to his discussions of metaphysics. Ernest Holmes attributes twenty-five percent of the Science of Mind philosophy to Troward's influence.

Studying and reading Troward brought Ernest Holmes ever closer to his creation of Spiritual Mind Treatment through all of his writings and the concept of the Power of our Thought/Word acting on Law.

> *"Every creation carries its own mathematics along with it. You cannot create anything without at the same time creating its relation to*

everything else, just as in painting a landscape, the contour you give to the trees will determine that of the sky. Therefore, whenever you create anything, you thereby start a train of causation which will work out in strict accordance with the sort of thought that started it. The stream always has the quality of its source.

Thought which is in line with the Unity of the Great Whole will produce correspondingly harmonious results, and Thought which is disruptive of the great Principle of Unity will produce correspondingly disruptive results — hence all the trouble and confusion in the world. Our Thought is perfectly free, and we can use it either constructively or destructively as we choose; but the immutable Law of Sequence will not permit us to plant a thought of one kind and make it bear fruit of another."[36]

CHAPTER 8:
MARY BAKER EDDY AND CHRISTIAN SCIENCE

Mary Patterson, as she was known at birth, spent much of her childhood and much of her adult life sick. Although she was steeped in the Bible and the ideas of God's power to heal, she continued to search for a way to heal herself of her ill health.

She was led to Phineas Quimby whose healing method freed her of invalidism and pain. It is said that the change was instantaneous, and "...within a week she climbed the one-hundred eighty-two steps to the dome of the City Hall."[37]

Mary Baker Eddy became very interested in Quimby's method of healing and studied his manuscripts. She lectured on healing in Maine, calling it "P.P. Quimby's Spiritual Science."

After Quimby's death in 1866, she injured herself in a fall and became a cripple again. Everyone thought she would die, but after reading about one of Jesus' healings she was said to have felt a healing presence. She healed herself through her own interpretation of Quimby's method. She said of her abilities: "I think that I could help another in my condition if they had not placed their intelligence in matter."[38]

Mrs. Eddy continued to teach the new ideas and methods as one of Quimby's followers until the period of her more public work. She called her method 'Christian Science,' and she started teaching classes in healing.

There was a plagiarism controversy over the origins of the manuscript on healing that Mary Baker Eddy wrote and whether or not she had stolen it from Quimby's writings. Finally, in 1875 she published her book, Science and Health. She claimed this philosophy of healing as her own discovery. The plagiarism controversy was subdued, but never really settled.

Quimby's son George Quimby made this public statement:

> *"As far as the book Science and Health is concerned, Mrs. Eddy had no access to father's manuscripts [save 'Questions and Answers'] when she wrote it, but that she did have a very full knowledge of his ideas and beliefs is also true. The religion which she teaches certainly is hers, for which I cannot be too thankful; for I should be loath to go down to my grave feeling that my father was in any way connected with Christian Science. That she got her inspiration*

and idea from father is beyond question. In other words, had there been no Dr. Quimby there would have been no Mrs. Eddy. Father claimed to believe, and taught and practiced his belief, that disease was a mental condition and was an invention of man . . . caused by error or beliefs, and capable of being cured mentally without medicine or appliances or applications—these ideas are embodied in Mrs. Eddy's book—she certainly heard father teach years before she wrote her book."[39]

This is the method of healing Mary Baker Eddy used and it is said there is no real difference between it and Phineas Quimby's method:

Removing fear in the patient, by explaining the mental cause of the illness.

Replacing the fear with faith and expectation to be healed.

Well if there would have been no Christian Science with Phineas Quimby, there might have been no Spiritual Mind Treatment without the influence of Mary Baker Eddy on Ernest Holmes.

From 1908 to 1910, while working in a grocery store, Ernest Holmes attended the Leland Powers School of Expression in Boston. One of the instructors was a Christian Scientist who gave him a copy of Science and Health with Key to the Scriptures by Mary Baker Eddy. He was intrigued with their concept of prayer.

"The most important result of his study of Emerson and Mrs. Eddy, he said, was that he now knew that 'God is good.' Until this time he viewed God as passive, not active. Now I believed He (God) was working at it and you could go along with Him. 'I intuitively felt that the affirmation of God's goodness would heal the sick. I began with the belief that God is all and I never departed from it.'

While Christian Science was important to Holmes, he never joined the church. He believed in its major principles, deeply respected Mrs. Eddy and her movement, and always defended her against criticism..."[40]

Although there are major differences between Science of Mind and Christian Science, there are major similarities that directly relate to Spiritual Mind Treatment.

Christian Scientists believe it is God's Love that heals. No one or no problem is beyond healing. Healing can be experienced in the here and now by everyone. Science of Mind teaches that the one Power is good. All healing takes place with the revelation of this Truth in Spiritual Mind Treatment

In Christian Science treatment, they do not plead with God. They do not believe in suffering or that it has any part in God's will. God is entirely good and his will for everyone is only health and life. In Science of Mind treatment, the practitioner affirms the Truth. There is no pleading or begging. The Will of God is always good.

Christian Science has trained practitioners who devote themselves to healing others through prayer. They do not offer counseling, diagnosis or any physical manipulation only, treatment as taught by Mary Baker Eddy Science and Health with Key to the Scriptures. Science of Mind has trained practitioners who devote themselves to healing others through Spiritual Mind Treatment. They do not offer counseling, diagnosis or any physical manipulation, they merely know the Truth.

It can be concluded that Ernest Holmes' introduction to Mary Baker Eddy's Science and Health was a very large step toward the development of Spiritual Mind Treatment and its five steps.

CHAPTER 9:
EMMA CURTIS HOPKINS

Emma Curtis Hopkins was born in Connecticut in 1853. She was educated at Woodstock Academy and remained there for a time as an instructor.

In 1882, she was healed of an illness by Mary Baker Eddy. Emma Curtis devoted herself to the study of Christian Science. She became a practitioner and served as editor (1884-85) of the Christian Science Journal.

However, it is said that Emma Curtis was a strong-willed woman and so was Mrs. Eddy. And so, their diverging opinions regarding truth led to their parting of ways.

In 1886, Emma Curtis left Mrs. Eddy, moved to Chicago, and established on her own the Christian Science Theological Seminary in 1887. There she taught the truth similar to Mrs. Eddy's and lectured, teaching classes in New York, San Francisco, Kansas

City, Boston and many other places.

She not only drew upon the Bible, but later included in her philosophy and teachings the non-Christian scriptures and the works of the world's great philosophers as well. She spent time in London, where she had contact with Thomas Troward and other British leaders of the New Thought movement. She eventually ceased using the name 'Christian Science' and began teaching privately.

Because of her considerable influence on the New Thought organizations, Emma Curtis Hopkins came to be called the "Teacher of Teachers." Her students and followers became the leaders of New Thought. They included Malinda Cramer and Nona Brooks, who co-founded the Church of Divine Science, Charles and Myrtle Fillmore, who founded the Unity School of Christianity, and Ernest Holmes, founder of Religious Science.

Emma Curtis Hopkins was a mystic. She emphasized this element in all her teachings and writing. She drew upon the Bible, the non-Christian scriptures, and the works of the world's great philosophers and saints in her teaching. Her mysticism was a very potent influence upon Ernest Holmes.

In her greatest work, The Twelve Powers of the

Soul, she wrote:

> *"Never the spirit was born,*
> *the spirit shall cease to be never.*
> *Changeless the spirit remains,*
> *Birthless and deathless forever."*

Emma Curtis Hopkins knew that it was by contemplating and embodying one's eternal nature that healing took place.

During 1924, Holmes had traveled to New York City to study with Emma Curtis Hopkins. Although his studies lasted for less than a year, Hopkins's impact on the development of his work was significant. It is said his study with Hopkins likely inspired the establishment of the Institute, which would later become the Church of Religious Science.

Holmes said of Emma Curtis Hopkins:

> *"I was fortunate to have been able to take her lessons on mysticism. She had transcendence about her that you could feel. It was really there…she was an illumined soul."*[41]

Ernest Holmes credited Hopkins with introducing him to the "limitless possibilities of practical mysticism." He thought that she was the only person who combined mysticism with the use of metaphysical healing."[42]

It seems that perhaps Emma Curtis Hopkins was the visible proof and walking example of someone who truly embodied Principle. Perhaps Emma Curtis Hopkins was the visible manifestation of what trained thought can do.

CHAPTER 10:
SPIRITUAL MIND TREATMENT

"To learn how to think is to learn how to live."

In Open at the Top, Neal Vahle quotes Ernest Holmes as saying,

"The Science of Mind is the Science of right thinking...The Law of Mind when rightly used irresistibly draws us toward the object of our desires. One of the most comforting ideas ever entertained was that thought could be used creatively to produce good in our lives."[43]

As has been written in this book, Ernest Holmes studied many of the great metaphysicians, healers and philosophers. However, he finally developed his own system of prayer. Ernest Holmes was indeed a mystic himself, but he also wanted to put to practice that which he knew as Truth.

This writer concludes that the creation of Spiritual Mind Treatment was divinely intuited through Ernest

Holmes as a practical method of assisting one in training his or her thought. Holmes developed Spiritual Mind Treatment as a practical tool to allow one to use the Law of Mind to change his outward experience and thereby improve his conditions.

Holmes defined Treatment as

"the science of inducing within the mind concepts, acceptance and realizations of peace, poise, power and plenty, health happiness, and success—or whatever the particular need may be. When we treat we do something to our minds to convert them to a new belief: from a belief in evil to a belief in good, from a belief in lack to a belief in abundance, from a belief in fear to faith."[44]

Ernest Holmes' form of prayer was a five step process that he encouraged all to use:

- The first step or Recognition is to recognize that there is an Infinite Power in the Universe that is only good.

- The second step or Unification unites the one praying with this Infinite Power. Ernest Holmes reminds the one praying that it is not enough to recognize that there is one Power if one does not know it as his own Power. One must pray in this manner, "There is one Life. This life is my life now."

- The third step is "Realization" or "Declaration."

Holmes called it voicing in thought what we desire. "…The Declaration should be definite, clear and specific…This establishes the desire as an entity in the realm of causation."[45]

- The fourth step is "Gratitude." This step must be heartfelt and real. It is an acceptance that the Declaration has been acted upon by Law and is already done.

- The fifth step is "Release." There is nothing else to do now but release the prayer to the Law, with the faith that it is done. Ernest Holmes wrote: "If our prayers are released as Jesus' were with the fullest confidence that the Law can do nothing else but answer, our demonstration will come thick and fast."[46]

Although the earlier healers mostly used prayer for the purpose of physical healing, Ernest Holmes felt that life was meant to be lived in fullness and joy, and that we should treat for anything that we wish.

"Does the thing I wish to do express more life, more happiness, more peace to myself, and at the same time harm no one? If it does, it is right. It is not selfish. But if it is done at the expense of anyone, then in such degree we are making wrong use of the Law."[47]

CHAPTER 11:
CONCLUSION

*"Science of Mind is a practical Science meant
for practical application leading to proof."*

Ernest Holmes writes:

*"Theories are fine but meaningless except for
idle speculation unless we practically apply
them to any and all problems and situations
that may confront us. It is wonderful to say
we believe in prayer, but what can it mean to
us unless we pray. There comes a time in our
process and growth where we must start using
what we have learned. Otherwise we can find
ourselves spending a lifetime gathering together
ideas which will be just a mass of interesting
information with no practical value."*[48]

Ernest Holmes spent a lifetime gathering ideas, but
he also found a way to use them for himself and to
share their practical use with the world. He called the
Science of Mind a "philosophy, a faith and a way of

life."

We can learn the philosophy. Then we must have faith in it. Lastly, we must use it in our lives. Without any one of these three things, it is not truly Science of Mind. Ernest Holmes meant for us to know that we could have wonderful, loving and fulfilling lives. He left us with the tool to reveal the Truth within ourselves and others: Spiritual Mind Treatment

ACKNOWLEDGMENTS

My eternal love, respect and gratitude go to Rev. James Mellon for being the one who has driven home the knowing that I am one with God, more bluntly stated, "I am God!" I also would like to thank him for being my greatest teacher and for inspiring me in the greatest way a leader can inspire, which is through example. Thank you, Rev. James, for always walking your talk.

Upon arriving at the NoHo Arts Center for New Thought, I came from the mentorship of Dr. Marlene Morris, whom I would also like to thank. Her purity of Spirit always saw the Divine in me. Her love allowed me the opportunity to blossom and grow at one of the most difficult times in my life. I have finally come to understand what she meant by the statement, "I'm in love with God," as I, too, have fallen in love with the Divine within me.

I would also like to acknowledge Richard Morgan, RScP, my first Science of Mind teacher who challenged me when I was only a short six months into this philosophy to become a practitioner. From him, I carry with me the most enduring lesson: it is done unto me as I believe I deserve.

To my fellow revs, Colette, Jay, Terry, James H, Sharon, Doug, Barbara, Gary, Jamie, Jonathan, and Sandra: Being able to walk next to you along this sometimes treacherous path has given me strength that I will always carry with me. Your powerful minds have expanded mine.

And of course, I would like to acknowledge my husband and fellow minister, Patrick Feren. He introduced me to this Science a short twelve years ago. He has not only been an emotional and intellectual support, but he has joined me on this journey. We are the ying and yang together. I love you, Paddykins!

To Ernest S. Holmes, I say thank you a million times for your great inspired mind and for dedicating your life to bridging the way from man to God. "Perfect God! Perfect Man! Perfect Being!" Thank you for that, and for knowing that "trained thought is more powerful than untrained thought," — and, for not stopping there, but also giving us the practical tool by which to change our thought and of which this paper is about: Spiritual Mind Treatment.

QUICK REFERENCE LIST

1 Vahle, Neal; *Open At The Top*

2 Holmes, Ernest; *Science of Mind, The*

3 Holmes, Fenwicke, *Ernest Holmes: His Life and Times*

4 *http://ernestholmes.wwwhubs.com*

5 Armore, Reginald; *That Was Ernest*

6 Vahle, Neal; *Open At The Top*

7 Vahle, Neal; *Open At The Top*

8 Holmes, Ernest; *Cosmic Consciousness Experience, Ernest Holmes' last talk.*

9 Holmes, Ernest; *Science of Mind, The*

10 Holmes, Ernest; *Science of Mind, The*

11 *John 10:30*

12 Holmes, Ernest; *Science of Mind, The*

13 *Matt. 8:18*

14 Holmes, Ernest; *Science of Mind, The*

15 Science of Mind Magazine Oct. 1982, p 20

16 *Luke 5:13*

17 Holmes, Ernest; *Science of Mind, The*

18 *Mark 8:6*

19 Anton Mesmer, from Wikipedia online

20 Chaffin, Jeffrey Michael; *The New Thought Movement, an Analysis and Comparison to 1st and 2nd Century Christianity.* p 3

21 *http://www.anton-mesmer.com*

22 Braden, Charles S. (1963); *Spirits In Rebellion*

23 Holmes, Ernest; *Science of Mind, The*

24 *http://thinkingiscausative.com/great-thinkers/ past-great-thinkers/97-ernest-holmes.html*

25 Quimby, Phinneas; *Quimby Manuscripts, The* [Ed. Horatio Dresser]

26 Holmes, Ernest; *Science of Mind, The*

27 Quimby, Phinneas; *Quimby Manuscripts, The* [Ed. Horatio Dresser]

28 *http://thinkingiscausative.com/great-thinkers/ past-great-thinkers/97-ernest-holmes.html*

29 Holmes, Fenwicke; *Ernest Holmes: His Life and Times*

30 Emerson, Ralph Waldo; *Self Reliance*

31 Holmes, Fenwicke; *Ernest Holmes: His Life and Times*

32 Holmes, Fenwicke; *Ernest Holmes: His Life and Times*

33 Holmes, Ernest; *Science of Mind, The*

34 Holmes, Fenwicke; *Ernest Holmes: His Life and Times*

35 Holmes, Fenwicke; *Ernest Holmes: His Life and Times*

36 Troward, Thomas; *The Law and the Word*

37 *http://marybakereddy.wwwhubs.com*

38 *http://marybakereddy.wwwhubs.com*

THIS THING CALLED TREATMENT

40   Vahle, Neal; *Open At The Top (69)*

41   Vahle, Neal; *Open At The Top (41)*

42   Vahle, Neal; *Open At The Top (78)*

43   Vahle, Neal; *Open At The Top (14)*

44   Vahle, Neal; *Open At The Top (14)*

45   Vahle, Neal; *Open At The Top (14)*

46   Science of Mind Magazine, 1982

47   Holmes, Ernest; *Science of Mind, The* (270)

48   Science of Mind Magazine, 1982

COMPLETE REFERENCES

Armor, Reginald C. (1999) That was Ernest. DeVorss and Company, CA: Marina del Rey.

Braden, Charles S. (1963). Spirits in Rebellion: The Rise and Development of New Thought (6th Printing 1980). Southern University Methodist Press, TX: Dallas.

Chaffin, Jeffrey Michael. The New Thought Movement, an Analysis and Comparison to 1st and 2nd Century Christianity. http://www. newthoughtcrs.org/archive/nt_movement.pdf

Carruthers, Martyn. The Quimby Connection: Model of a Healer http://www.soulwork.net/sw_articles_eng/quimby.html

Creativelife.org. Creative Life Spiritual Center. Ernest Holmes Biography, http://www. creativelife.org/holmesbio.html.

Dresser, Horatio W. (1961). The Quimby Manuscripts (edited by Horatio Dresser from the notebooks of Phineas Quimby 1846-65). Citadel Press, NJ: Seacaucus.

Emerson, Ralph Waldo (1926). Essays by Ralph Waldo Emerson. Harper and Row Publishers, NY: New York.

Holmes, Ernest S. (1959) Cosmic Consciousness

Experience. (reprinted with corrections from The Anatomy of Healing Prayer, compiled by George P. Bendall.) CA: Whittier.

Holmes, Ernest S. (1919). Creative Mind and Success. Robert M. McBride & Company, NY: New York

Holmes, Ernest S. (1984). Living the Science of Mind. Devorss and Company, CA: Marina del Rey.

Holmes, Ernest S. (1955). Seminar Lectures (Revised) by George C. Maxwell, Editor, Science of Mind Publications, CA, Los Angeles.

Holmes, Ernest S. (1938). The Science of Mind, (2nd ed.. Penguin Putnam Inc., NY: New York.

Holmes, Ernest S. (1943). This Thing Called Life. G.P. Putnam's Sons, NY: New York

Holmes, Fenwicke L. (1970). Ernest Holmes: His Life and Times

Hopkins, Emma Curtis (2006). Class Lessons of 1888. Wise Woman Press, OR: Beaverton.

Ousley, Jr., Stan. Authentic Divine Science for Real People An Introduction to the Basics. Symphony of Love Ministries. http://www.angelfire.com/wi2/ULCds/SOL-ds-basics.html NM: Santa Fe

Troward, Thomas (1909). The Edinburgh Lectures

on Mental Science. Thomas Troward (printed in the U.S.) Dodd Mead and Company, NY: New York.

Vahle, Neal (1993). Open At The Top, The Life of Ernest Holmes. Open View Press, CA: Mill Valley

http://ernestholmes.wwwhubs.com/

http://thinkingiscausative.com/great-thinkers/past-great-thinkers/97-ernest-holmes.html

Science of Mind Magazine, July 1982

About the Author

Rev. Rita Andriello-Feren is a licensed minister and practitioner with the Centers for Spiritual Living, a world-wide Spiritual organization based in New Thought philosophy and the teachings of Ernest Holmes. Rev. Rita has over two decades of experience in teaching, curriculum development, writing, workshop development and implementation, theater and music, management and business. She began her ministerial career in 2012, serving as Assistant Minister and Administrator at The NoHo Arts Center for New Thought in California. Rev. Rita's Assistant Ministry included Pastoral Care and Outreach. Her Outreach ministries included the labyrinth, a prison ministry and volunteer work at L.A. Family Housing. In 2013, she moved to Kaua'i with her husband Rev. Patrick Feren and they founded the Center for Spiritual Living Kaua'i, which is a now a thriving center with a membership of over 150. Her life's mission is to awaken each and every person to their Magnificence through self-love.

*See the CSL Kaua'i website: www.cslkauai.org
or contact Rev. Rita at 808-755-9177*

Made in the USA
San Bernardino, CA
29 November 2018